CHILDREN IN CHINA

CHILDREN IN CHINA

Text and Photos by Michael Karhausen

ORBIS BOOKS

Maryknoll, New York 10545

The Catholic Foreign Mission Society of America (Maryknoll) recruits and trains people for overseas missionary service. Through Orbis Books, Maryknoll aims to foster the international dialogue that is essential to mission. The books published, however, reflect the opinions of their authors and are not meant to represent the official position of the society.

Orbis/ISBN 0-57075-144-7

CONTENTS

To those who work for mutual understanding and respect
between China and other nations.

There's an old Talmudic teaching which says that every child is born with a message to deliver to the human race . . . a few words, maybe a work of art, maybe a bench he'll build, maybe something he'll say that completes the explanation of why we're here.

Sam Levenson, U.S. humorist

AN ANCIENT LAND OF YOUTH

 *Chinese call their homeland* Zhongguo. *The character* zhong *means "middle" and* guo *means "country." Since ancient times the Chinese have considered their country the center of the world—the "Middle Kingdom."*

Twenty-five years ago China was another world. For most people in the West, it was a potential enemy. Closed off from most of the world, it had a long complicated history and difficult-to-pronounce names for people and places. Since then China and the rest of the world have drawn closer together, but increased contacts through business people, tourists, journalists, scholars and students sometimes leave Westerners even more confused than before about the giant of Asia.

We admire China's ancient philosophies, arts and medicine, yet its political system and some of its values remain alien to much that Westerners hold dear. We oscillate between images of the Great Wall and Tiananmen Square. Lost in the images are the people—one-fourth of us human beings alive today who are Chinese.

Where can we begin to meet the Chinese people who are the inheritors of an ancient culture and the bearers of that tradition into the next millennium? Children offer an attractive and powerful medium through which to learn. Whether the cause be biological or spiritual or some combination of the two, children draw us to themselves in ways that their elders do not. When we see them, we do not think of politics, economics or history. Children demand that we see them as people. When we do so, we begin to engage their culture not as an abstraction, but as something embodied in this girl, that boy.

The Union of Catholic Asian News, an agency based in Hong Kong that reports news of and for the Catholic church in Asia, commissioned photojournalist Michael Karhausen to spend two years with children in China in order to learn about their country. Karhausen's impressions and photos form the basis of *Children in China*. The final text was prepared by Barbara Baker, Madeleine Marie Slavic and William J. Grimm, M.M.

If this book enables you to see the Chinese people and their homeland as part of your own world, if the children you see here become in some sense your own children, then *Children in China* will have achieved its purpose: to build the connections we need with each other in order to create a more peaceful future for the children of China and the whole world.

中國

Children bring out the best in people: the squawking voices of elderly women take on cuddly tones, tattooed men puffing on dangling cigarettes want to hold the infant on their shoulders, and perfect strangers become bearers of friendly advice—or, on a bad day, blunt scoldings.

Child labor is not uncommon, but it is officially illegal for children under the age of sixteen to work in China. The National People's Congress, the parliament of the People's Republic of China, has passed many other laws concerning children, including prohibiting corporal punishment in school, child abuse in the home and child marriages.

Chinese law requires schooling for nine years, but many children do not get a full education. Of the 600 million people who have had schooling, over half only attended elementary school.

Tractors are unknown to many Chinese farmers, who plow their fields with hoes or water buffalo. Children in rural areas, as here in Inner Mongolia, are often expected to lend their young muscles to the hard work.

Buses in China's cities are likely to be extremely crowded, so get on at an early stop! Once aboard, you'll hear a cacophony of polite and impolite horns: bus drivers are legally required to announce their presence to cyclists, who fill city streets with their own clangorous chimes.

Siblings, like these six-year-old twins named Meng Jiao and Meng Yao, frequently have the same first character (word) in their two-character given names. Traditionally, however, sons and daughters are often called by their position within the family: elder sister, number two brother, little son and so on.

A nurse measures a young boy. Height varies considerably in China: Northerners tend to be taller and bigger-boned, while people in the South are likely to have slighter frames.

Haircuts are commonly provided by sidewalk barbers. For those lucky enough to go to a barbershop, however, relaxing hot towels are placed on your face after the haircut, and a soothing head massage may be included at no extra charge!

A child of the 1990s in Shenzhen, one of China's four special economic zones. In economic areas where flexible tactics have been introduced to encourage foreign investment, lifestyles change quickly because the latest trends accompany the infusion of money.

SOCIETY'S CHILD

 The character chung *means both "loyalty" and "patriotism." It is made up of a heart below a pictogram of an arrow piercing the center of a target. This shows that loyalty—whether to country, person or principle—needs a properly centered heart.*

What is it that makes a child Chinese, American, Mexican or Korean? It is belonging, being shaped by a culture, that makes one a child of that culture. Each of us is a "Society's Child." Where does the society come from that makes the children in these photos Chinese? What are its roots?

One of the first legends children in China hear is the story of Pan Gu, creator of the world. In the beginning there was a big egg. In the middle of the egg lay the sleeping giant Pan Gu. After 18,000 years, Pan Gu woke up and swung a huge axe, splitting the egg in two. The egg exploded and the light, bright pieces rose higher and higher to become heaven, while the heavy dark pieces fell and formed the earth. For the next 18,000 years Pan Gu stood like a pillar, with hands raised, holding heaven and earth apart. Finally, he was so exhausted that he died, and when this happened his skull became the heavens; one eye the moon and the other the sun; his body became the five holy mountains of China and his soul was inherited by humankind.

Who is the first famous non-legendary figure in Chinese history? Many Chinese would probably answer Qin Shihuang, the first emperor, who ruled from 221 to 207 BCE and began construction on the Great Wall of China. The early dynasties saw much internal conflict, but the Sui Dynasty (589-618 CE) managed to establish a degree of order by strengthening the civil service and updating the legal code. The Tang Dynasty (618-907), one of the most glorious of all, is noted for its painters, scholars and poets. Weakened by wars, the Tang fell to the Song Dynasty (960-1279), which is remembered for its commercial revolution, including the introduction of paper money.

Chinese rule in China ended when Kublai Khan and his Mongol army conquered the country and established the Yuan Dynasty (1279-1368). Power eventually reverted to the Chinese under a rebel leader named Hongwu. Under the new Ming dynasty (1368-1644), China developed into a strong maritime country, but corruption, coupled with wars and famine, brought about a huge rebellion that led to the last of the dynasties, the Manchu-led Qing (1644-1912). The first century of Manchu rule was prosperous, but as time passed, the inward-looking government could not stimulate the technological and scientific growth that countries elsewhere were enjoying.

In 1911 a revolutionary movement under the Western-trained doctor Sun Yatsen declared China a republic. Under Sun, two political movements, Nationalism and Communism, competed for power. After Sun's death in 1925, Chiang Kaishek controlled the Nationalist Party, and eight years later his army encircled the Communists, who made their "Long March" from the south to the north. In 1937 the Japanese marched into China and fought until 1945. After World War II, the Japanese were expelled and the Communists took power after defeating the Nationalists. In 1949 the Communist leader Mao Zedong proclaimed the People's Republic of China and became its first president. The Nationalists set up a rival government on the island of Taiwan.

Mao inherited a bankrupt country. Over the next two decades, he launched many plans, movements and campaigns to carry the nation forward. While much progress was made during Mao's revolutionary-spirited rule, most Chinese now acknowledge that he also made many mistakes, the gravest being the "Great Leap Forward," which led to famines that killed tens of millions of people, and the Cultural Revolution from 1966 to 1976 when the Party sought to cleanse society of people and things that were considered "feudal," "capitalistic" or "bourgeois." Much of China's heritage was destroyed: temples, monasteries, churches, paintings, musical instruments and books.

Soon after Mao's death in 1976 his long-time opponent Deng Xiaoping came to power. Deng's priority was economic growth, and he moved China toward further integration into the world economic system. By the mid-1990s China had succeeded in becoming the fastest-growing economy in the world, though vast poverty remains. Though Deng died in 1997, his "to get rich is glorious" move toward market capitalism continues, and the Communist Party retains control.

A major challenge for Deng was the nation-wide student uprising in 1989. Thousands of students gathered in Tiananmen Square, a large public square in Beijing, to protest against inflation, corruption and the slow pace of political and social reform. On June 4, after a month of demonstrations by the students and their supporters, some 350,000 troops of the People's Liberation Army put an end to the much publicized student movement. People throughout the world watched the demonstrations and their violent suppression on television.

Though the students challenged the Communist regime, throughout China many children between the ages of seven and fourteen still wear the red scarves that signify membership in the Chinese Young Pioneers. These are distinguished students, model children honored by the Communist Party. Founded in 1949, the organization provides its members (around 130 million) with activities similar to those of the Boy or Girl Scouts. Since 1982 all children from elementary school onwards can become members and wear the red scarf or, if they are too young, a green scarf. To become a member, a child has to know and follow the Pioneers' principles: love and respect for the motherland, people, labor, science and public property.

Young Pioneers are also encouraged to follow the example of Lei Feng, a Communist hero. Some people say Lei Feng never really lived, others that he was born to a poor family in 1940 in Hunan Province. His grandfather, father, brothers and mother all died before he was seven, but he still went to school, studied hard and graduated with excellent results. He was a Young Pioneer who wore his red scarf with honor. Later he joined the People's Liberation Army and became a model soldier and leader. In the 1960s and 1970s, every Young Pioneer read stories about Lei Feng, and though he is not so popular in China today, the legendary hero is still well known by most children.

For children who are disappointed at having to leave the Young Pioneers and for those who became interested in politics at a later stage, there is the Communist Youth League of China for youths between fourteen and eighteen. Founded in 1922, one year after the Communist Party of China, it has over 58 million members and honors young people with titles such as "Youth Hero." On May 4, Chinese Youth Day, new members are accepted all over the country and are educated to become supporters of the Party.

Since 1984, the Young Pioneers have been represented in the National People's Congress, the parliament of the People's Republic of China. In 1991 the NPC passed a series of laws on child welfare that ordered at least nine years of mandatory education, gave protection against child abuse in the home and corporal punishment in school, forbade parental discrimination against handicapped children or girls and prohibited child labor under the age of sixteen. Child marriages, child kidnaping and the trading of children were also made illegal.

Though religion is often seen by the Communist government of China as superstition, and only atheists are permitted to be members of the Communist Party, religious traditions have always had a strong influence on Chinese life. The constitution guarantees freedom of "normal religious activity," but religious bodies may not be subject to foreign domination, and all religious activities must be registered.

Children may grow up with many different religious influences. Among the folk religions of China, animism, which attributes a living soul to plants, inanimate objects and natural phenomena, is mixed with elements of Taoism and Buddhism. There are numerous gods honored by the Chinese, such as Po Sheng, the God of Medicine, and Tsai Shin, the God of Wealth. Ancestor veneration is also part of folk religion and during past dynasties nearly every village had its own ancestral temple, many of which were destroyed during the Cultural Revolution.

Taoism is the only uniquely Chinese religion. Its history goes back to Lao Tse, whose name means "Great Old Master." He was born around 604 BCE. According to legend, his mother was pregnant with him for 82 years. So when he was born, he was already an old man with the wisdom that comes with age. At the end of his life he is said to have climbed on a water buffalo and ridden west in search of solitude. On the way he was stopped by a guard who asked him to give evidence of his beliefs, so he wrote the book *Tao Te Ching* before continuing on his journey. *Tao* means "way," and Taoism emphasizes meditation and following a way of life in harmony with nature.

In the quiet town of Qufu in Shandong Province in eastern China, large numbers of the inhabitants are named Kong, after Kong Fuzi (Confucius) who was born there. Up to three-quarters of the townspeople claim to be descended from the sage. Confucianism, often said to be more of a philosophy than a religion, has influenced the social life in China from 400 BCE, and for decades it was the official state doctrine. Banned under Communist rule because it was thought to be synonymous with the old feudal China, Confucian teachings are once more gaining influence.

Buddhism came to China from India in the first century CE. Buddhist monasteries and temples sprang up everywhere. Monasteries acted as guesthouses, hospitals and orphanages as well as money-lending enterprises and pawn shops. Buddhism is also experiencing a resurgence as ruined temples are being rebuilt throughout the country.

Records of Jews settling in China extend back to the year 950, but today there are only a few descendants living in the eastern part of China in Kaifeng. Islam came through Arabian merchants in the seventh century and spread primarily to millions of Hui minority people. Although Muslims are found all over China, the largest concentration is in the northwest. In cities like Hohhot, Xi'an and Beijing mosques have received large subsidies for restoration, and are very active.

Christianity first came to China in the seventh century, when a Syrian named Raban presented Christian scriptures to the imperial court in Xi'an. Later, in the fourteenth century, Franciscan missionaries arrived in China. In the succeeding centuries, other Catholic missioners came, including Matteo Ricci and other Jesuits famed for their contributions to Chinese culture. In the 1950s the Communist government expelled foreign missionaries, confiscated churches and founded Chinese Christian churches, loyal to the state. Today, there are an estimated 100 million religious believers in mainland China. Although official estimates list around 11 million Christians, unofficial figures put the number as high as 40 million as Christianity continues to grow.

忠

These boys perform on Children's Day wearing the red scarves of the Young Pioneers, whom the Communist Party of China honors as distinguished students and model children. As Young Pioneers (there are around 130 million), they must love and respect their motherland, people, labor, science and public property.

The number of visitors to mainland China has exploded in recent decades. There were only 1.8 million in 1978, but in 1996, 51 million tourists visited China. Despite the increasing presence of foreigners, children are still curious when they see someone from another country, especially one with a camera.

Children gathering for kindergarten in Shanghai. Today education for all children is a priority throughout China. Children are required to attend school from the age of seven for at least nine years.

These days, it is more usual to see a boy than a girl child in China. In the future, this imbalance means a man will have a harder time finding a woman to marry.

On October 1, 1949, Communist leader Mao Zedong proclaimed the People's Republic of China and became its first president. He inherited a bankrupt country and went on to make much progress but also many mistakes.

A boy drawing in an art class at the Nanjing City Ninha Middle School. Nanjing is home to a prestigious art school and child painters from Nanjing exhibit their work throughout China.

Children selling watermelons in the Shenzhen Special Economic Zone, bordering Hong Kong. The billboard of Deng Xiaoping, who died in February 1997, says, "Be persistent with the fundamental Party line. It will not be shaken for a hundred years."

In Nanjing, a four-year-old boy visits a Catholic shrine with his mother and grandmother. Christianity first came to China in the seventh century, and despite conflicts with the Communist government, it is officially estimated that mainland China has 11 million Christians. However, unofficial figures put the number as high as 40 million.

Buddhism, Confucianism and Taoism all have their own temples where people worship, make offerings and teach their children to do the same. This Taoist temple in Hong Kong honors Wong Tai Sin, who many believe cures illnesses and grants horse-racing tips.

The one-child-per-family policy may leave a youngster feeling spoiled or deeply obligated. It may also ensure that the parents have enough money to properly feed and clothe their solitary offspring, as well as have the time needed to make the child feel happy, loved and cared for.

Shanghai provides some of China's most progressive activities for children. Satellite dishes dot the municipality's roof tops. Several youth magazines are published here. This city of more than 12 million people also boasts of having a children's art theater, over seventy children's palaces and its own film animation studio.

A boy in front of a model of Tobet's Potala Palace in the Cultural Village in Shenzhen, a special economic zone just across the border from Hong Kong. The Cultural Village is a popular tourist attraction.

THE PRECIOUS CHILD

 Zi *means "child." The character originally showed an infant with arms and legs extended, then it changed to a baby swaddled in pieces of cloth.*

Chinese say a newborn child is so fragile that even a breath of wind can disfigure its face. Since there are evil spirits about, children wear embroidered tigers on their shoes, hats and collars as protection. The coiled tiger can leap out of the fabric and devour an enemy at a moment's notice. An embroidered cat will pounce on a rat that dares approach a sleeping infant. A decorative rooster scares off nighttime demons with its loud morning crow.

Only the closest relatives may visit a newborn during the first days of life. On the third day, northern Chinese wash the baby's head with a potion of herbs and prickly ash to get rid of demons as well as to bless the child with good fortune. When the infant reaches its first month and is out of the worst danger, the family might rejoice with a "full-moon" celebration to thank the watchful gods. In this ritual, held on the night of the life-giving full moon, the child's head is shaved. The soft hair is placed in a small bag sewn with red and green threads, and hung in the family's ancestral hall. The hair becomes a little spirit in the home.

Children are traditionally thought to hold supernatural powers. In ancient times, villagers would listen carefully to what a young child might sing, as the lyrics could proclaim an oracle for the family, village, county or province.

A parent might say a child is like wood. To raise a child well is like carving the wood with great care and precision; when the carving is finished, the child is great to behold. But until that time, the undeveloped child is an incomplete adult with little or no personality of its own, a shapeless block of wood. In fact, to some Chinese, a child's death is not seen to be as tragic as the death of an adult. The dead child, it is believed, had the soul of a person to whom the family owed something, and when that debt was paid through the parents' love and care, the child died.

Debt and duty. These two concepts remain deep within Chinese culture, especially in the doctrines of Confucianism. Through proverbs and folk stories, at school and at home, in theaters and in temples, Confucius and his followers have taught a strict social hierarchy: children bow to the will of their parents, the wife to the husband, the younger to the elder and the subject to the ruler. This emphasis on position permeates the home, as children are often called by their place in the family, such as "elder sister" or "second eldest brother," instead of by their given names. Confucius also believed that filial piety was the key to harmony in the family, and the "correct" relationship between parent and child is reflected in the Chinese character for "piety": the character shows the ideogram of an "elder" above that of a baby.

Under the long rule of Mao Zedong the family lost some of its importance. From the Communist point of view, children were now state property and were taught to give their highest allegiance to the country and the Party. Wearing their bright red scarves, young children sang songs such as, "The love for my father, the love for my mother, cannot compare to my love for Chairman Mao."

In 1982 the duties of parenting were written into China's highest law, the Constitution of the People's Republic of China. Article 49 states that parents must raise their children, a principle which could easily be taken for granted, but it means that the government is freed of the financial burden of providing for over 300 million people under the age of fifteen.

Traditionally, parenting in China follows certain patterns: the father is strict and the mother kind. "It is easy to reign over a kingdom, but difficult to rule a family," a saying goes, and one character for father includes the character for "stick" as a symbol of the father's authority. It is also a general rule, reinforced by government education campaigns, that children should never be left alone.

In every culture children are taught to be on their best behavior, but in Chinese society children who disobey bring great shame to the entire family. Children learn early that the family is greater than one individual person, child or adult.

That children must respect their parents and help them in their old age is also written in the Constitution. Traditionally, this care continues in the afterlife, too, when children bring rice, meat and fruit to their parents' and ancestors' graves to offer respect and to "feed" them in the next world. However, only sons can properly honor a family's dead ancestors, and only sons are able to continue the family line. A great fear for many parents is that of turning into "hungry ghosts" after death, roaming the world in agony and loneliness, with no sons to care for them.

When a son is born, he is honored. Traditionally, a wooden bow is hung at the left of the family's doorway, symbolizing that the birth is as noble as the heavens. The newborn son can sleep on a bed, wear good clothing and is given a piece of jade in respect. For a girl, the celebrations are subdued. A handkerchief is placed at the right of the doorway to show that the female infant is as ordinary as the earth. Wrapped in strips of rough cloth, she sleeps on the ground and is given only a simple small tile. The patriarchy of China's society permeates everything—even the character for "good" combines the characters "woman" and "son," not "daughter" or "child."

A son is valuable, yet vulnerable. To protect a precious baby son from being kidnaped by ghosts, parents may first give their son the name of an animal or a girl, and then later give him his real name. An animal is not worth harming and traditionally a girl is seen as negligible. In rural areas, daughters are sometimes called "goods on which one loses money" or, along with handicapped children, "maggots in the rice." Farmers naturally prefer strong sons who will work hard in the fields. Girls are also seen to be expensive.

With a daughter, all the fruits of child-raising disappear, for as soon as the girl gets married, she leaves her parents' household to serve her new parents-in-law.

In 1979 China introduced a one-child-per-family policy, a birth-control program for the nation. While the international standard for birth rates is 105 boys born for every 100 girls, China's birth rate stands at 114 boys to 100 girls, reflecting the cultural preference for boys. In Shandong Province the birth rate reaches 163.8 boys to 100 girls. In an effort to prevent this imbalance from continuing, in 1995 China outlawed the use of ultrasound technology to identify the sex of a child before birth, a practice that led to the abortion of unwanted pregnancies. Even so, it is estimated that as many as one million baby girls are being abandoned each year.

The government calls the new family system the "four-two-one-family": four grandparents, two parents and one child. With fewer children in each family, they will be better educated and will enjoy a better standard of living than their parents. In a country where over 70 million of the 1.2 billion people live in poverty and where there are 20 million new babies each year, limiting the number of children is a major concern of the state.

How is this one-child policy being enforced? In the past, pre-pubescent pairing of children in marriage was done by parents and matchmakers. Sometimes a young boy was married to a woman who first served as his babysitter. Since 1994, however, women must be over twenty years old to marry, and men must be twenty-two; and couples are asked to delay having children. Once married, couples receive free contraceptives, and after their first birth, sterilization is encouraged. About ten million Chinese are sterilized each year and, according to the Chinese government, there are ten million abortions a year. About 25 percent of Chinese women have had an abortion.

Most city people have only one child and wealthier families have created a generation of single children called "China's Little Emperors"—well-treated, sometimes spoiled children who do not have to share things with brothers and sisters and often get exactly what they want. The extended family—the-four-two-one plus aunts and uncles—dotes on the child; there was actually a case of a six-year-old "emperor" who was not able to dress himself.

But the life of this "royalty" isn't all glory and comfort. Children shoulder great pressure from parents who have invested in piano lessons, computer courses or language schools for their heirs and heiresses. Huge expectations of success weigh upon children, and some cope badly, becoming depressed or aggressive. Drug abuse is beginning to appear among China's children.

Healthy or otherwise, more and more of these children are emphasizing their individuality. Selfishness and egoism are two very non-traditional Chinese traits, and the government and schools are trying to overcome this situation by encouraging children to be modest, to share with others and to pay respect to their parents instead of being served by them.

On the other end of China's wide spectrum are "black-list children," illegal second- or third-born children. These unregistered children, more common in the countryside where farmers depend on as many children as possible to work in the fields, cannot go to school unless their parents send them to private schools, which are rare and expensive. These children, their numbers unknown, also have no access to state-provided medical treatment.

Most of the black-list children stay home. They feed the pigs and chickens every morning, walk into the hills to fetch water in bamboo pipes or clay jars and do their share of grinding the family grain by hand. They are as precious as jade as they help their family, day after day.

Are the penalties of having a second child an effective deterrent? If caught with a second child, parents can pay fines and lose government privileges. Sometimes property is confiscated from a poor family who cannot afford to pay the fine. But some parents choose to pay the fine, especially for a son. One family nicknamed their boy, "Color TV," an expensive yet enjoyable addition to the family!

子

In traditional rural society, girls are sometimes called "maggots in the rice" or "goods for which one loses money." Not so with these two girls, whose names Yu Huan (left) and Luo Yu mean "joy" and "jade."

On Children's Day, boys and girls become larger than life. This young boy has been transformed into a classical scholar proficient in calligraphy, literature and Confucian philosophy.

The pipa (a lute with four strings) might be an ancient instrument, but it is not forgotten.

The international standard birth rate is 105 boys for every 100 girls, but the ratio of boys to girls in the People's Republic is 114 to 100. A law enacted in 1995 now forbids doctors from using ultrasound to determine the sex of an unborn fetus.

A girl in Hohhot (Blue City) in Mongolia. Crisp blue skies are children's companions here in one of China's sunniest regions. Mongolians traditionally see the sky as holy. Shamanism and nature worship are still practiced by some of China's 56 ethnic minority groups.

A bouquet of freshly picked flowers goes to this lucky boy, while the girl proudly wears a medal.

Honoring the ancestors is an important part of life in China and even young children are taught these rituals by their parents. In the past nearly every village had its own ancestor temple, but many of these were destroyed during the Cultural Revolution.

Children in China help their families with much of the work, whether it's toiling in rice paddies or bringing goods to the town market. Illiteracy can be high in the rural areas where children are an important source of labor and have no time, and often no funds, to go to school.

Japanese-style comics reach far beyond Japan. The action- and often violence-packed cartoons are popular with children.

The Chinese government calls the new one-child-per-family system the "four-two-one family": four grandparents, two parents, one child. This grandfather and toddler visit with a broom maker.

The sight of two brothers can be uncommon in today's China. What are the penalties for having a second child? Parents may pay fines and lose government privileges, or else have property confiscated in lieu of payment.

Life for a child in Mongolia can mean snow on sand dunes. On a summer evening, you can see your own breath. Because schools in parts of Mongolia are closed for the winter owing to the extreme cold, students go to school longer during the summer.

The general parenting rule of rarely leaving children alone is reinforced by government education programs in China. Groups are an integral part of social and socialist life, from childhood through adulthood.

A Chinese person probably would say that the people of China have black eyes and black hair, whereas many Westerners would be inclined to say Chinese have brown eyes and black hair.

A young ballerina wearing a jade necklace. According to Taoists, a young child is as precious as jade. Millions upon millions of Chinese wear the stone in necklaces, rings and bracelets. Jade symbolizes purity, nobility and beauty.

GAMES, POEMS AND STORIES

風箏 *The Chinese word for "kite" is made up of* feng *meaning "wind" and* zheng, *which is a stringed instrument similar to a zither. Toward the end of the Tang Dynasty (618-907 CE), silk strings or bamboo pipes were fitted onto kites so that they made music as they flew in the wind.*

Tops, tumblers and kites originated centuries ago and are still used by children today. Tops were traditionally made of wood, clay, bamboo or stone. Tumblers of clay, wood or papier-maché are shaped like babies, old men, officials and animals, with a weight in a semi-spherical base. However hard a child pushes them over, they roll back to a standing position. Kites were originally used for forecasting the weather and for military purposes, but since the Tang Dynasty they have been flown for fun. At first they were made of richly decorated paper or silk stretched over bamboo frames. Now they come in every possible shape, size and color and can be seen flying in large squares, such as Tiananmen in Beijing.

There was no concept of "doll" in China until the nineteenth century, when true dolls, elaborately dressed in Chinese style, with detailed faces and separate limbs, were designed and manufactured. During the last hundred years, children in China have also played with stuffed toys, building blocks, kaleidoscopes and toy weapons. Today almost every toy imaginable is available in the cities, from simple dominoes to sophisticated computers, but children still devise their own games, or play international ones such as hide-and-seek or tug-of-war.

It is only very recently that the importance of play in a child's development has been recognized in China. The word for play is *wan*, part of *wanhu*, which means "to neglect." *Wan* is also part of the saying *wan wu sang zhi*, which means "if you are occupied with useless things you will lose your determination." Traditionally it was believed that a child who learns a great deal can expect a good future and will bring honor to the family, but a child who plays does not learn. In 1991, however, Premier Li Peng signed a declaration saying that not only education, but also the situation of children's play should be improved.

Many parents hold the attitude that books are better than toys. For decades, children in China have been told stories and poems about the actions and behavior of characters that children can follow as moral examples. Some of these poems are published in *The Three-Character Classic*, a book so named because each line only has three characters. This book is seven hundred years old, but remains popular today. In 1990 it was recommended by UNESCO as a book of moral education for children. Here are four examples of the classic poems:

A jade stone, uncarved, unpolished with care
Can't turn itself into fine jade ware;
If man refuses to learn, he will likewise
Be ignorant of hows and whys.

Huang Xiang of nine, for his parents old,
With his own body warmed up the bed-mat cold;
Such filial piety, a model of this kind,
Should always be borne firmly in mind.

A child of four, Kong Rong was modest,
He let his brothers choose the best pears first.
This norm of love fraternal, bear in mind:
Between brothers, be polite and kind.

There are yet other examples to follow,
Such as reading by bagged fireflies' glow,
Or learning by the glimmering white snow:
Too poor for lamp, yet of books they ne'er let go.

While China's rapid economic development has changed many traditions, some ancient legends continued to influence children. For instance, a very popular cartoon series for children is "The Journey to the West," which is based on a sixteenth-century novel that tells the story of the Buddhist monk Xuan Zang, a historical person who is said to have made a fantastic expedition with the Monkey God, Sun Wukong. It tells how the Monkey God, who is worshiped in China, comes to earth and protects the monk by defeating ghosts and evil spirits.

Children's heros, though, are not limited to traditional literary characters. Mi Qi Lao Shu and Tang Lao Ya, "Old Mouse Mi" and "Old Duck Tang," known in the West as Mickey Mouse and Donald Duck, are also popular.

風箏

The importance of play in a child's development has only recently been officially recognized in China. Children's spare time is still more likely to be spent at a children's palace, learning skills such as calligraphy or dancing. And even in dance, extraordinary precision and coordination are taught.

Lessons often influence play, and many "games" in fact are formal. Moreover, many dances and songs have the theme of labor running through them. The Chinese traditionally have seen themselves as producers—not consumers—but this is changing fast.

Two boys wrestle on the steppes of Inner Mongolia. The art of fighting is a national sport in China, with competitions every year. Some of the many styles involve fighting with hands or fists, but swords or other weapons are also used. One technique especially popular with children is "long boxing," which relies particularly on speed and dexterity.

Archery is also a traditional sport in Inner Mongolia. During summers on the grasslands, festivals that feature riding games, wrestling and archery can be a welcome diversion for the nomads, who travel from one pasture to another, living in round tents called yurts.

Play in rural areas is often confined to school vacation, when one of the most popular recreational activities for children is fishing. The anticipation is great as they walk to the river's edge and spend some hours by the water, especially with the added excitement of possibly catching supper.

How sweet it is to go home after school. Children smile and play spontaneously along a dirt road in Inner Mongolia.

Apart from textbooks, school children also read stories and poems with Confucian ethics and moral teachings, which provide examples for them to follow.

Modern forms of play still sometimes use traditionally popular animals such as the monkey. The Monkey God Sun Wukong was first worshiped in China in the sixteenth century. Now his story is seen by children in a popular television cartoon series.

Reverie in play. This five-year-old Mongolian boy has a keyboard. Leisure time is changing.

FOOD FOR THOUGHT

 The Chinese word for "cooked rice" is fan. *The character consists of the root "food" and the phonetic element "returning." "Returning" symbolizes the repeated movement of the hand picking up the food with chopsticks, passing it from the bowl into the mouth.*

Confucius once said, "The joy of food is the first happiness." Much of people's thinking in China revolves around food, and it plays an integral part of many aspects of daily life. Children are often rewarded with special dishes and Western-style sweets when they behave well. Traditionally, they receive a painted red egg on their birthday, as red symbolizes happiness and the egg is a sign of life. Families like to discuss food—where they can find the best and the cheapest restaurants, which markets offer food of the highest quality, and which ingredients create the most delicious meal.

Chinese do not like to eat alone, and family life mainly takes place during meals at home. Going out for lunch or dinner enhances a family's reputation, and banquets in particular reflect social status. Poor families may host an opulent feast for a special occasion such as the birth of a child, a wedding or a funeral, while wealthy families have banquets more frequently. In former times, when there were guests in the house, children often sat at a separate table in order not to disturb the adults. Nowadays with the single-child policy, children are dressed in their best clothes and enjoy the beautifully present-ed food alongside the adults.

Children who grow up in different parts of China eat different food, the best known cuisines being Cantonese (south), Shanghai (east), Mongolian (far north), Sichuan-Hunan (west and central) and Beijing (northeast). Cantonese cooking is probably the most familiar in the West, and includes lightly cooked delicacies such as steamed fish and *dim sum* dumplings. Shanghai food is often accompanied by a soy sauce and brown sugar mix, making it slightly sweet. The predominant influence in Mongolian cooking is Muslim, with lamb and shish kebab as specialities. The Sichuan-Hunan area is drizzly and foggy, and its cuisine, with its hot peppers and flaming sauces, is supposed to be a counterpoint to the climate. Beijing is often a mixture of all these cuisines, but is most famous for its crispy Beijing (Peking) Duck.

North of the Yangtze River (which flows from Sichuan Province in the west all the way to the China Sea) a meal will almost certainly include noodles. South of the river, meals include a steaming bowl of rice. In southern China the importance of rice in the diet and culture is shown in the language. The phrase "to eat" is *chi fan*, literally, "eat rice." If somebody loses his job, people in China say that "his rice bowl is broken." As the staple food, rice is so valuable that children are often taught never to leave any grains of rice in their bowl when they have finished a meal.

Children learn to handle chopsticks gradually. At first they hold them in their fists. After a while, they grab them near the bottom. In the course of time their hand moves higher and higher until one day it looks quite elegant. To make eating easier for chil-dren, their chopsticks are only about seven inches long, instead of the usual nine- to eleven-inch ones used by adults. Eating a meal with chopsticks is different from eating with a knife and fork: everyone selects food from dishes in the middle of the table. Every dish is for everybody. In Chinese cuisine meat and vegetables are chopped into numer-ous bite-sized pieces. Meat near the bone is considered the tastiest, so the meat is cut so that as many pieces as possible contain a bit of bone.

Not all children in China, however, have good food to eat. In rural areas 40 percent of children under seven suffer from anemia and iron deficiency. In the cities, on the other hand, some children eat too much and have to go on diets. There have been terrible famines in Chinese history, which may be one reason the Chinese have learned to eat things that may seem strange to outsiders. In the course of time the Chinese have developed many dishes with chicken's feet, snakes, scorpions, dogs and cats. Another reason could be superstition. In ancient times people thought that eating an animal's kidney or brain, for example, might strengthen their own equivalent organ.

Tea is the traditional beverage, even for children. Since ancient times tea has been considered a medicine because it is prepared with hot water and is thought to protect people from illness. There is no precise distinction between food and medicine in China. Chinese medicine developed independently from Western medicine, which focuses on the source of the disease. Instead, Chinese medicine focuses on the whole person and reflects the pursuit of the *yin/yang* balance that imbues much of Chinese philosophy. *Yin* and *yang*, simply defined, are opposites such as male and female, hot and cold. The Chinese believe that when the miniature cosmos of the body suffers an imbalance of its finely-tuned forces—for example, too much heat—the body succumbs to ailments.

Traditional medical treatment has remained largely unchanged over the centuries. If a child has a cold, it is thought that the body's harmony of hot and cold is disturbed. The remedy is to eat food with cooling properties, such as green vegetables, tofu and melon. Just as some foods cool the body and some foods like nuts, garlic and snake heat it, some are nutritious and some "poisonous." Fish, carrots, ginseng and many foods that are red in color are considered especially nutritious. Crab meat, goose and pheasant, on the other hand, can be "poisonous." This doesn't mean these foods are dangerous; a healthy person can eat them, but an ill person should not because they can make the illness worse. Other dishes are thought to be "non-nutritious." They are the meat of animals like the octopus that are regarded as unemotional because they lack red blood or tears. Other traditions exist, too; for example, children suffering from measles or smallpox should avoid sesame because the shape of the seeds is reminiscent of skin diseases.

Food is also an important part of Chinese festivals, the foremost of which is Chinese New Year, which falls between January 21 and February 19, depending on the lunar calendar. Shortly before New Year's, children help clean the house, getting rid of the old year's dust along with its shortcomings and disappointments. It is a time to buy new clothes for the family. On New Year's eve, the highlight of the festival, the whole family gathers at home for a festive dinner when seven different kinds of vegetables are served. Children stay up late in their fancy clothes, with red a favorite color. They receive *hongbao*, small red envelopes containing "lucky money." Elder people bless the younger, and the new year is welcomed with the explosive sound of firecrackers. Small children may be a little fearful, older ones delighted, but most important, demons are frightened away.

As the days of the festival proceed, dishes with symbolic meaning are prepared. For example, in the South, dried oysters with hairy seaweed (a hairlike plant from the Gobi) are eaten to bring prosperity in business and good fortune. Pork and bean sprouts represent wealth, while tangerines bring luck, and fish a surplus. Meanwhile in Hubei Province in central China, rice and cassia flower pudding are served to ensure a sweet year.

There are many other festivals. On the fifth day of the fifth moon (usually falling in late May or early June) is the *Duanwu* or Dragon Boat Festival, when children enjoy rice dumplings made in memory of Qu Yuan. A statesman and poet, Qu Yuan became one of China's most celebrated martyrs, when in 278 BCE he sacrificed his life by drowning himself in the Mi Lo River in Hunan Province to protest the corrupt government. When the local villagers heard what had happened, they jumped into their boats, paddled frantically, and threw glutinous rice dumplings into the water so that the sea dragons would not eat Qu Yuan. Now rice dumplings are eaten by the people, but young and old alike watch spectacular dragon boat races in which competitors furiously ply their oars in a symbolic search for the body of Qu Yuan. What watching child would not want to grow up to be one of those brightly clad rowers?

The Moon or Mid-autumn Festival is also fun for children. On this day when the moon is considered to be most beautiful, people traditionally climb mountains and hills to welcome it. Children are the leaders as they carry candle-lit lanterns shaped like fruit, animals and fish. In the past, the lanterns were made of paper but nowadays they are often plastic and are sometimes lit by a battery-operated bulb. The traditional food of this festival is mooncakes, which are round pastries filled with lotus seed or red bean paste and sometimes one or more egg yolks. The heavy, glazed mooncakes are so sweet and rich that children often only need to eat a small slice to last them until the next year.

飯

Life in rural China can be hard for old and young alike: the health care system is inadequate, winter severe, and food often scarce. Even in Beijing, sometimes during the winter cabbage may be the only fresh vegetable at the market.

Much of life in China's cities happens on the sidewalk, as in Guangzhou (Canton), China's southern commercial center. You can find some of the best Cantonese food cooked at a small *dai-pai-dong* and served on a folding table. Pull up a stool!

The child is often the center of attention at meal time. To make eating easier, a child's chopsticks are only seven inches long; those of adults are nine to eleven inches.

Cooking is an art, performed with care even in humble circumstances. When food is cut in small pieces, it requires less cooking and saves fuel—hence the development of Chinese cuisine. The names of everyday dishes often reflect the way the meat or vegetables are cut—in strips, cubes or slices.

A family meal often begins with cold vegetables and pickled meat, followed by hot foods of contrasting tastes and colors, even including sweet dishes. Rice is eaten during the entire meal, and the meal usually ends with soup.

Until quite recently, China was repeatedly ravaged by famine. Some children still do not have enough to eat or the variety of food they may crave.

For the Mid-autumn or Moon Festival, children stay up late and light candles in parks and on mountains. Their private or shared pleasure can be as intense as that of American children who "trick or treat" on Halloween.

A child is examined by a nurse on Children's Day. More normally, school children are covered by the school's medical service. Children under the age of one are examined free every three months. Youngsters up to seven years of age generally see a doctor less often, but still at least once a year.

What will this Mongolian girl, living in a tent, have to eat on the now empty table? Unlike southern China, rice is not the staple food in the North. Instead, wheat products such as noodles and dumplings predominate and large amounts of onion and garlic are used, but there is little variety.

Grandmother and child may eat very differently. The Chinese traditionally do not eat milk products but growing numbers of the young do, though cows are few in number due to the shortage of grazing land. As Western food becomes more available in Chinese cities, it attains popularity with the young generation.

A noodle vendor is helped by her daughter as patrons sit at cramped tables to enjoy one of the nation's communal pastimes—eating. Small open-air food stalls abound throughout China.

PEIJUN, A VILLAGE BOY

 The Chinese word for "learning" is xue. *It signifies a teacher laying hands crosswise upon dark clouds that cover the mind of the student.*

Peijun gets up at five o'clock in the cold, wet morning. Squatting, he brushes his teeth with hot water in his rice bowl, then rushes back into the sleeping room, climbs onto a chair and lifts a basket from the wardrobe. Under a bunch of wool he finds his treasure—four marbles.

In the kitchen, two big woks stand heating on the fire. Peijun's mother and father are already preparing lunch and dinner, cutting meat and vegetables into many small pieces and frying them in hot oil. The family can afford to eat meat at least once a day, but for many Chinese families meat is too expensive. They can eat only rice or noodles with vegetables and tofu, which is made from bean curd and referred to as "meat for the poor." Peijun's mother and grandmother run a small clinic in the village, and Peijun's father is a farmer, so they are well off.

It's time for breakfast. Peijun gobbles down rice and vegetables, then takes his school bag and hurries to school. Most of the people in Peijun's village are farmers. Peijun walks past fertile green rice terraces. He takes the trail that leads to the school building where the Chinese flag flaps in the wind, and some girls are sweeping the playground.

Peijun's classmates are all carrying small sticks with dangling plastic bags. The village doctor is visiting the school today, and all the children have to bring in their stool samples to be examined. Everybody, that is, except Peijun, because his mother and grandmother run a clinic and can take care of his health themselves.

Class starts with eye massage. Every day in Chinese schools children massage their eyes, which may account for the fact that there are comparatively fewer children with glasses in China than in Western countries. Six hours of lessons make up the school day. In the first lesson, the students learn Chinese characters. China has many languages, but each one uses the same written characters. There are 70,000 different characters, but school children have to learn only 2,000 to 3,000 in order to read a newspaper or book. Every day Peijun learns at least six new characters. The teacher writes a new Chinese character on the blackboard, counting the strokes while the children copy. Children also have to learn the characters in Western form, called *pinyin*, which allows people to write Chinese with the Roman alphabet.

Mathematics is the second main subject at school. Peijun is only seven, but each day he and his classmates have to tackle thirty-one problems. Children are also taught singing, natural science and physical education, and, in later grades, Chinese geography and history. Peijun's next lesson is moral education. This day the children look at two pictures in a school book—one of the pictures shows a clean table, the other a dirty one. Then the students discuss which table gives a better impression and why.

Lunch break. The children run to the playground. They play the eagle game where one child is the eagle, and the rest are chickens. Again and again the eagle tries to catch the chickens. Next they play the tiger game in which the tiger tries to catch the little pig in the middle of the circle. But the pig is protected by a wall of other players. Xu Fong, one of Peijun's older schoolmates, is the eagle as well as the tiger. He is an outstanding student whose favorite subject at school is Chinese. His hobbies are ping-pong and television, especially children's programs and war movies.

A clanging sound is heard over the shouts of the children all over the playground. The teacher is standing on the wooden veranda banging a rusty pipe against the pillar of the school building. The children rush into the classrooms, sit down at their clumsy desks and rummage for their exercise books. They all start to read, every child a different text. The squeaky voices mix like chirping birds. Then the children have an art lesson and have to draw a "new lady," a species of beetle. At the end of the day, there is a test. Finally Peijun can go home.

A few children, however, stay behind to clean the classroom. Others go home to prepare dinner for their parents and brothers and sisters. Peijun goes to fetch water, has dinner, does his homework and goes to bed between eight and nine o'clock. Children's play is not encouraged by adults in China, so most children in rural areas find time to play only during vacations. Summer vacation lasts two months. In some regions, the school day finishes earlier during harvest time to enable the children to help their parents in the fields. In parts of Inner Mongolia, there is no school during winter because of the cold. Instead, students go to school longer in the summer.

During the vacation in Peijun's village, the children catch insects, build small dams in the river or go fishing. Some children have electronic games such as small electrical pianos or Gameboys. If he has any spare time, Peijun likes to play with his marbles and watch television, especially cartoons. He doesn't talk to friends on the telephone because, like most people in China, he does not have a telephone. In some rural areas, one thousand people have to share two lines.

Though it is illegal for a child not to go to school from the age of seven for at least nine years, not all children in China go to school. Some cannot afford the school fees of about 55 yuan ($7) for half a year. Some children help their parents in the fields and many girls work in the home. In 1949, about 80 percent of Chinese people were illiterate. By 1994 the figure was 12.5 percent. This is still 200 million people, most of whom live in the countryside. If he goes to high school, Peijun will study agriculture, and when he is older, he will probably be a farmer and work in the rice fields with his father.

Xiao Peijun, whose name means "virtuous soldier," stands while sharing a hurried meal with his cousin, Duan Yu. For breakfast, they eat yesterday's leftovers of rice, vegetables and, these days, often meat. Poorer families who cannot afford meat instead eat tofu—bean curd.

Setting off at dawn, children like Peijun and his neighbor may walk long distances to school. The paths they take cut through farmland soon to be worked by their parents.

After a walk through rice paddies, a child rests at the flagpole outside his school. In village and city alike, flag raising and singing the national anthem are an integral part of school life.

Children with expectant smiles crowd to get into the school room. But education in China is not always rewarded. A skilled worker can earn more money than an academic and most children do not finish upper secondary school. Only a few get through the rigid state college entrance examination.

At busy times, there is no class for children in the countryside, where the extreme pressure and competitiveness typical of school life in urban areas is much reduced. Students from rural backgrounds are allowed into university with lower scores on entrance exams, but are less likely to advance so far.

Peijun's grandmother, Dr. Wang Yuxian, runs a clinic. She is using acupuncture to treat six-year-old Qing. Ear acupuncture, a new form of the treatment, has recently been developed. Instead of needles, it involves using small seed kernels, which are massaged onto certain points of the ear by the patient.

Not a normal "school bag" for these children. Inside the plastic bags are their stool samples, which will be examined by a village doctor visiting their school that day.

Not only do children clean the playground in the cold morning air, they also help clean their classrooms after school.

Eye massage is part of every school day. This may be one reason why comparatively fewer children in China wear glasses than in Western countries.

Books rather than toys are often given to children as presents. To read a newspaper or book, a child needs to know 2,000 to 3,000 of the Chinese language's 70,000 characters.

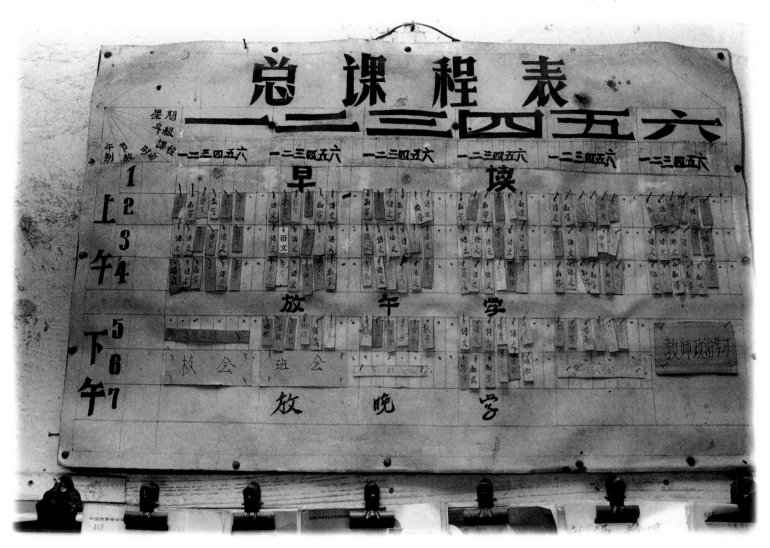

The school-day timetable has six hours of lessons. The main emphasis is on learning Chinese and mathematics, though young children are also taught science, moral education, art, singing and physical education. Chinese geography and history are added in later grades.

The eagle game is popular in the playground. One child is the eagle and the rest are chickens who form a line behind a hen. Again and again the eagle tries to catch the chickens. Chinese culture allows close physical contact among same-sex friends, whether children or adults. It is not uncommon to see women walking holding hands, or men arm-in-arm.

Xu Fong (middle), Peijun's friend, looks down proudly. He is the recipient of an award in school. Xu Fong says he wants to be a soldier when he grows up.

There are many contrasts between life in the village and life in an urban area and this is particularly true of opportunities for education. But while lessons may be harder to learn within the crumbling walls and poor facilities of some rural schools, there is still time for fun.

When the Chinese Republic was founded in 1949, about 80 percent of the population could not read or write. By 1994 illiteracy had been cut to 12.5 percent.

Xu Jie and his friend Wang Hun, both 14 years old, play Chinese chess, a game that dates back to the sixth century. The pieces are red and black cylinders—more like checkers than Western-style chess pieces. In the game, they are placed at intersections, not on the squares, of the black and white grid, which is usually made of paper.

Village life is quintessential to China. The whole family helps cultivate crops on every bit of their small plots.

SMALL CHILD, BIG CITY

 The Chinese word for electricity, dian, *is part of many other words: "cinema" translates as "electric shadow house," "telephone" is "electric talk," "television" is "electric vision" and "computer" is "electric brain."*

Monday morning, Shanghai. Children and their teachers line up in the playground. When the music starts, everybody exercises—a healthy way to start the school week. Then it's robust singing of the national anthem, followed by the principal's talk. As three proud, uniformed students raise the flag, a classmate explains to the assembly, "Why were these three chosen to have this honor? Because last week Zhang Geming made sure that each student had a lunch box; Bo Zhiwei cleaned the classroom thoroughly, even staying after school to do it; and when Zhang Lili had an operation and had to stay at home for six months to recuperate, she studied very hard and returned to school to excel in her examinations!"

Students in big cities like Shanghai probably benefit most from China's growing economy. While some rural schools are poorly lit, with broken desks and chairs and painted brick walls as blackboards, urban schools may have modern buildings with air-conditioned classrooms and athletic fields. A few privileged students attend schools for the gifted. Shanghai, for example, is home to a renowned conservatory of music to which only one out of a thousand applicants gains admission. Once there, the eight hundred prodigies practice their instruments at least five hours a day.

Meanwhile, talented child painters in Nanjing, encouraged by a prestigious art school in their city, exhibit their work not only throughout China, but internationally as well. Athletically gifted children train in Beijing, where strenuous coaching primes gymnasts for the Olympic Games.

Children's palaces are another unique urban attraction, institutions that offer courses for the six- to sixteen-year-old in a wide range of subjects: astronomy, knitting, kung fu, Morse code, music, computer science and just about everything between. Children practice their skills here for about ninety minutes a day. The first children's palace was established in Shanghai in 1953 by Song Qingling, the widow of Sun Yatsen, founder of the Chinese Republic; she saw these government-funded activities as a support to the education provided by schools and parents. The palaces, of which there are now over one thousand throughout the country, also aim to help students discover their talents and prepare them for future careers.

Walk into a children's palace and you are likely to see children copying characters written by famous calligraphers. You smell fresh ink throughout the rooms, and the walls are covered with calligraphy painted on delicate rice paper. In Wuxi, a city seventy-five miles from Shanghai, a calligraphy master teaches children this highly regarded ancient art, a discipline that many Chinese study their whole lives. Calligraphy masters say that the simpler the character is, the harder it is to write beautifully. For at least one hour a day, each student practices "the way of the pen." In the first exercise a young child traces characters over and over until the exact brush pressure is learned. If a student positions a character too high or too low on the page, or if the distance between the characters is not correct, the teacher might shout, "That's too narrow! Do you stand like that?," mimicking the character by pressing his arms against his body as if he were trapped in a tight sausage skin.

Wealthy Shanghai, the country's most populous city with twelve million people, probably provides the most progressive activities for a child of the 1990s. At least 5 percent of Shanghai families own a home computer. Satellite dishes dot roof tops, and children's stores offer a selection of the most modern toys available. Several youth magazines are published here, including *Little Gentleman*, which is produced by children. Shanghai also offers a children's art theater linked with the Chinese Institute of Welfare, and over seventy children's palaces. The city even has its own film animation studio, which is China's equivalent of Disneyworld.

But life in the big city—and thirty-five cities in China have more than one million people—is not without problems. There are reports of increasing suicide and drug abuse among urban youth. Six of the ten most polluted cities in the world are in China, and the flood of over 100 million people from poorer inland provinces to the booming cities of Guangzhou, Beijing and Shanghai makes for fierce competition, rising unemployment, youth gangs and street children.

A new urban problem of the 1990s is overeating. Whereas in former times famine and malnutrition were not uncommon and the best food was reserved for the elderly, nowadays children often receive the best and the most food. *The China Daily*, the official government newspaper, reported a mother bringing her child to a kindergarten and telling the teacher that her child only ate chocolate, milk, pig's liver, and spicy pork with sauce. All other food, she claimed, had less nutritional value. "The Chinese have always liked to express their wealth through food, especially in the feeding of their children," explains one doctor who has opened a weight-loss camp for children. She says that many children became overweight by eating too much fast food such as hamburgers, french fries and ice cream. A seventeen-year-old Shanghai boy holds the national record for losing the most weight—154 pounds.

In the fever of China's growing capitalistic economy, Article 43 of the Chinese Constitution reminds people that, "Working people in the People's Republic of China have the right to rest." This means children, too. To this end, more than 60,000 video halls and 200,000 discos, ballrooms and karaoke clubs have opened in the past fifteen years. *The China Daily* writes that karaoke is "all the rage because it offers an opportunity for everyone . . . to cut loose and have a good time." One youth foundation donated 10,000 karaoke sets to youth centers, one of the largest recent projects "aimed at improving the cultural life of the youth and children."

On the family level, parents who can afford to may buy their children computers or electronic games. Color televisions in their homes offer entertainment that includes "Ultraman," a popular import from Japan. Children from poorer urban families may play table tennis or basketball, which most schools in China provide. Various forms of Chinese opera and the circus are two traditional and inexpensive forms of entertainment that the whole family might also enjoy.

By the mid-1990s the gap between the rich and the poor in China was the largest in the world. In the rural southwest, for instance, many families struggle for clean water and enough to eat, while in the coastal areas, special economic zones, and along the Yangtze and Yellow rivers, a higher standard of living can mean children in designer clothes from Hong Kong being driven around in luxury cars by the family chauffeur.

In the recent past, children were raised not only by their families, but also by the work unit or neighborhood committee—two community-oriented administrative bodies. The work unit could be a factory, a hospital, a university or a ministry, and every worker's family belonged to one. Children went to the unit's school from kindergarten through high school, and the sense of belonging to a group was very strong. In urban residential districts, the neighborhood committee looked after families who moved into the area. The committee settled quarrels among neighbors and even helped find jobs for young school drop-outs. Nowadays, private business people don't belong to a work unit, and every family in the new housing developments lives on its own—the work unit and neighborhood committee are fading away, and personal responsibility has arrived.

Nearly every city block in China has at least one construction site: skyscrapers, shops and restaurants. Urban areas have experienced extraordinary changes in a phenomenally short time.

With computers at their fingertips and cellular phones to their ears, many children living in the cities now have access to resources and influences undreamed of by their forebears. With the growth of one-child families and the decline in communal responsibility for their upbringing, they have a freedom or license that is new to China. How these young people grow up, the adults they become, will shape the world of the twenty-first century.

電

Art in China is traditionally composed of calligraphy, painting and poetry, together known as the "three perfections." For thousands of years artists have combined the three within a single painting, filling white skies with poetry written in their best calligraphy. Nowadays, youngsters are also exposed to more Western artistic expression.

Music crosses a huge spectrum in China. Children perform nationalistic songs wearing their Young Pioneer red scarves; at dawn in city squares people of all ages learn ballroom dancing accompanied by blasting boom boxes; a clash of cymbals brings one into the Chinese opera hall filled with people drinking tea and sharing bowls of peanuts. In clubs and discos, however, heavy metal and rock 'n' roll are being reinvented, Chinese-style.

The accordion is found not only across the laps of young students in classrooms, but also in the arms of poor street performers, often with a pet monkey in tow.

This 21-string zheng is one of many ancient musical instruments. Others include traditional Chinese-style flutes, lutes, violas, piccolos, trumpets and ceremonial gongs.

At least 5 percent of families in Shanghai already own a computer, which the Chinese language literally calls an "electric brain." Computer manufacturing and assembly plants are typical new industrial developments in mainland China.

A children's palace in Shanghai, one of about one thousand such venues throughout the mainland. These often grand institutions offer courses for the six- to sixteen-year-old in a wide range of subjects, from computer science to music, kung fu to Morse code, and astronomy to knitting.

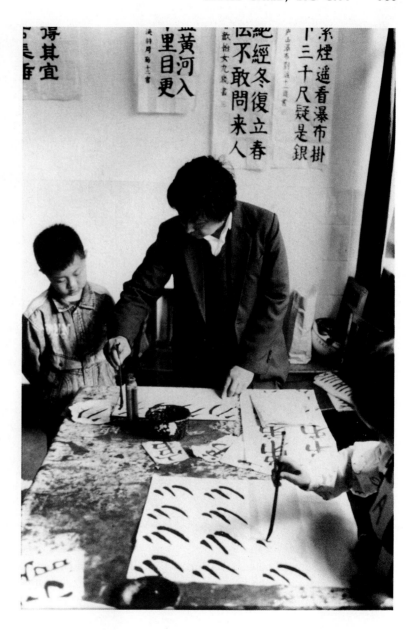

This young boy is learning calligraphy from a master calligrapher at a children's palace. A student will trace a character over and over until it is acceptable, painting with ink on delicate rice paper.

With about 25 percent of China's 1.2 billion people living in urban areas, many city children spend almost all their free time outside, since apartments can be small and dank in the cities. The rest of the population lives in villages, but many of those places are becoming so large that "village" does not fairly describe them.

Six of the world's ten most polluted cities are in mainland China. Other urban problems include rising unemployment, youth gangs and increasing numbers of street children. Over 100 million people from poorer inland provinces have flooded into China's booming cities, such as Beijing, Guangzhou and Shanghai.

As these school children grow older, they will face many challenges, including urbanization. In the mid-1990s Shanghai already has a population of twenty million and thirty-four other cities in China have populations of more than one million people.

New roads and highways are being built to meet the demands of China's economic growth. For example, a super-highway linking Guangzhou, Shenzhen and Zhuhai will be over seventy-five miles long when completed.

A policeman and his one-child family. The preference for a male child is common. According to tradition, only sons can continue the family line, and only sons can properly honor a family's dead ancestors. Patriarchy permeates everything in traditional Chinese society.

Yang Juan and her classmate Yu Yang, both six-year-old students in Sichuan Province, wave goodbye.

Epilogue

There are many things that make children in China different from children elsewhere. Chinese children eat different foods, learn different things and play different games from children in other lands. They are the products and heirs of centuries of a unique history and culture.

Even so, there are many things that make children in China not unlike children elsewhere. They have likes and dislikes in food; they rely upon grown-ups to teach them by word and example; they love to play. They can be endearing and irritating, hope-filled and fearful, competent and inept.

The attraction we feel toward the children of China pictured in this book is the same attraction we feel toward all children because, in a sense, all children belong to all of us. They are our responsibility in the present and our hope for the future.

Children are also ourselves because, no matter how old we become, part of each of us will always be the child we once were. Looking at children, we see something of the adults around them, including ourselves. Getting to know the children of China should give us a new openness to the adults of China. Like their children, the adults of China are different from adults elsewhere. They eat different foods, have different traditions, do different things. They are the products and heirs of their history and culture.

Even so, there are many things that make adults in China not unlike adults elsewhere. They have likes and dislikes; they have responsibilities they shirk or fulfill; they work and they play. They can be endearing and frustrating, hope-filled and fearful, competent and inept.

If China's children entice us to feel more at one with all China's people, we will have learned what it is that children all over the world have to teach us: that we are one family, attracted to one another unless or until "grown-up" politics, economics, culture, religion and philosophy interfere.

If we can meet all the world's people as we meet the world's children, we will have gone a long way to breaking down the barriers that divide our world. That will be the beginning of peace.